GRANDMAS

ARE ALL ABOUT

LOVE

All over the world, grandmothers are called by special names. They were mothers first, but now grandmas can take more time to do things they want to do.

Whether it has been a day, a week or more since we have seen her, she is always happy to see us. She loves to see us arrive and hates to see us leave.

From the time we are just babies, we feel comfort and love in our Grandma's arms.

She is good at keeping secrets. It is fun to know there are things only we both know.

Gabe has taken family
vacations before,
but he has never
traveled overni

RIDING
on a TRAIN

animals can
in the Western
Australia.
One for

OUT OF THE POUCH

Grandma reads the best stories and does lots of different voices. She loves to hear us read to her, too.

When we spend the night at Grandma's, she makes our favorite foods – like chocolate chip pancakes. Even better, she lets us help her cook and doesn't even mind if we make a mess.

       We like to go for walks with Grandma. She walks a little slower, and we love to look at the animals and birds and every flower as we walk.

Some Grandmas take us to the park, and we take turns pushing each other on the swing. Other Grandmas build sandcastles on the beach or they blow bubbles with us in the yard.

BLESS OUR HOME

We have lots of fun when we stay inside too. We do puzzles and play games. We love to paint and draw or play with dolls. Watching movies and eating popcorn is especially fun with Grandma.

Sometimes we need to rest, and Grandmas lies down with us. Other times, she just takes a snooze in her favorite chair.

Grandmas are so gentle when they brush our hair. We love polishing each other's nails, and grandmas don't mind if we get a little polish on their fingers too.

    Dancing with Grandma is always lots of fun. We usually end up giggling and acting just a little crazy.

Grandmas love to give and get kisses. Anytime, anywhere, they can never get too many kisses.

LAUGH~LOVE

Grandmas give the best hugs - especially when we have to say goodbye.

REPORT CARD
READING
MATH
SCIENCE
HISTORY
MUSIC
ART
PE
A
B+
A
B
A
A
D+

The best thing about Grandmas is we always know they are proud of us…

they will always love us –

no matter what!

There is no END

to a Grandma's love!

SOME OTHER NAMES FOR GRANDMA

Arabic- Jiddah (Shid-dah)

Cherokee – Agilisi (Ah-gey-lee-see)

Chinese – Nai Nai (Nigh-nigh)

English - Granny, Grams, Meemaw, Nana, Gigi, Gammy

Filipino – Lola (Loh-lah)

French – Grandmere (Gran-mare)

German and Dutch– Oma (Oh-ma)

Greek – YaYa (Yah-Yah)

Hawaiian – Tutu (Too-too)

Hebrew – Savta (Soft-tah)

India – Awa – (Ah-wah)

Italian – Nonna (Nah-nah)

Irish (Gaelic) – Maimeó (mam-o)

Japanese – Sobo (Soh-boh)

Korean – Halmoni (Hal-muh-nee)

Russian and Polish – Babushka (Bah-boosh-kah)

Spanish – Abuela (A-bwel-lah)

Swahili – Bibi (Bee-bee)

Swedish—Mormor